GWENNETH LEANE

The Sign
Messages for the Minute

ILLUSTRATED BY
KYLIE LEANE

PUBLISHER
Kylie Margaret Leane
kmlpublishing.com

COVER ART/DESIGN/ILLUSTRATIONS
Kylie Leane

© 2023 Gwenneth Leane
All rights reserved.

No portion of this publication may be reproduced or transmitted,
in any form or by any means, without the prior written permission of either copyright owner or publisher of this book.

THE SIGN: MESSAGES FOR THE MINUTE

Paperback Edition / September 2023 Gwenneth Leane
ISBN: 978-0-6451032-8-1

PRINTED IN AUSTRALIA

For information address:
gwen.leane@gmail.com
authorkylieleane@gmail.com

Gwenneth's Blog can be found online at:
www.wanderingwithwords.com

The Sign
Messages for the Minute

Do you feel God is a fable, a myth,
part of folklore? Are you searching for him?
Would you like to find him?
If you found God, what would you do with him?
Would you gladly become his beloved child,
or would you remain independent?
Would you hedge your bets and sit on the fence?

One thing to realise is:
"And it is impossible to please God without faith. Anyone who wants to come to him must believe that God exists and that he rewards those who sincerely seek him."

Hebrews 11: 6.
New Living Translation.

God is real;
the natural world around us attests to his reality.

The Psalmist writes,
"*The Heavens are telling the glory of God; they are a marvellous display of his craftsmanship. Day and night, they keep on talking about God. Without a sound or word, silent in the skies, their message reaches out to all the world.*"
Psalm 19: 1-4.
New Living Translation.

Who is God that we should believe in him?
God has called himself the *"Great I Am that I am"*.
Meaning God is, was and will be.
God is complete.

Another point is that God loves us beyond what
we know and understand as love.
We are his crowning creation,
and his love for us knows no bounds.

Did God slip up when he gave us free will?
In his eyes, no!
God wanted a people to choose him,
to love him of their own free choice.
God could have created us as puppets
where he pulled the strings,
and we had no option but to obey.

Adam and Eve in the
Garden of Eden faced a choice.
God said,
"You may eat any fruit in this Garden except fruit from the Tree of Conscience — for its fruit will open your eyes to make you aware of right and wrong, good and bad. If you eat its fruit you will be doomed to die."
Living Bible.
All was well in the Garden;
Adam and Eve walked with God and talked
with him each day in the evening.

Until the serpent came to them and hinted that
God had lied to them and that they would not die
but would become God if they ate it.
The snake hinted that God was withholding
crucial information from them.
The fruit looked delicious,
so Eve reached out and picked it,
and they both ate.

It was not until God came into the Garden that
evening for his usual chat that the couple
recognised they were naked and hid.
The eyes of their understanding was opened,
and they knew
right from wrong for the first time.
They knew something inside them had died.

Shock, horror, it was too late,
and a great chasm opened between
them and God.

Adam and Eve saw they had been equal with God,
had been God's beloved,
they'd had everything,
but now there was no way to recoup their losses.

To cut a long story short,
we are the offspring of Adam and Eve.
We are the inheritors of their scam.
We are living a life of separation from God
because of the tragic mistake made by
Adam and Eve.

Are we happy with our present lot?
Do we sometimes think about
God and wonder if he is real?
Are we aware of God?
Do we feel that God will somehow
come through for us?
Do we depend on our good deeds
to make God look at us favourably?
Do we want to regain all that Adam and Eve lost?
Do we want to enjoy walking and talking with
God as they did initially?
We can, you know.

Enter Jesus Christ, God's Son.
In these days he (God) has spoken to us
through his Son to whom he has given everything,
and through whom he made the world
and everything there is...
and all that God's Son is and does mark him as God.
In the New Testament,
God announced to the world that
"Jesus is my beloved Son,
and I am very pleased with him."

God sent Jesus to live amongst us
and be one with us to reveal God to us.
God accepts no other religious stream.
He has commissioned Jesus to be the one and
only who opens the door to intimacy with
himself.

*"There is salvation in no one else! God has given no
other name under heaven which will save us."*

Acts 4: 12
New Living Translation.

Jesus, God's only Son,
is responsible for restoring humanity to an intimate relationship with God,
as Adam and Eve
first experienced in the Garden of Eden.

It is about now that you are saying,
*"Whoa! Not so fast!
That is discrimination and intolerance.
What about Buddha, Islam and Baha'i and many other
streams of worship?
Surely, these groups lead to God?"*
Are you saying,
*"I have to believe in a God who is so narrow-minded and
one-eyed that he can't accept any other way?"*

These religious streams suit man's ego,
modify the behaviour, and give the devotee a false
sense of well-being.
These believers work at being good,
doing good, reinventing themselves,
living to earn God's favour.
In short, the follower must please
God by good behaviour,
by living up to the standard God has set.

Behind the thinking of any religion is the thought
that God is angry with us,
and we have to perform so he will be pleased
with us and not visit us with bad luck and,
in the end, grant us eternity based on the good
we have done.
It is a no-brainer to realise no one can ever reach
the mark God has set
for people to live by or maintain.

The truth is God is not angry with us.
If we read our Bible correctly,
we'll find that God loves us beyond, beyond.
God's love for us is not
condemnatory or judgemental.
Instead,
he seeks to lift us out of the darkness we live in.

We find that God wishes to bless us
abundantly beyond our wildest imaginations,
grant us health, provision and protection.
God desires our company;
he went to great lengths to regain our company
through Jesus' death and resurrection.
What more can he do to convince us of his
unconditional love for us?

A critical point in our deliberations is the story of
Nicodemus visiting Jesus by night;
here is part of their conversation,
"Jesus replied,
'I tell the truth, unless you are born again,
you cannot see the Kingdom of God."
John 3: 3; New Living translation.
Nicodemus said, *"How can a person be born again?"*

To answer Nicodemus's question,
we need to accept the death of Jesus Christ in
payment for our enmity, ignorance
and independence against God.
We need to turn around and live for God
and not ourselves anymore.
We need to Jesus to come into our heart and life.

Jesus accepted God's punishment and
anger that should have been ours.
In other words, Jesus became us and
was punished as us so that we could
go free when we accepted
Jesus Christ as Lord and Saviour.

"For God made Christ,
who never sinned, to be the offering for sin,
so that we could be made right with
God through Christ."

2 Corinthians 5: 21; New Living Translation.
Through believing in Jesus and acceptance of
Jesus we are born again.

Accept Jesus as saviour,
and Jesus will infuse us with himself.
Our inner person or spirit
will be renewed or born again.
We are then new people.
Being born again is more than just getting into
heaven when we die.
Jesus died to give us eternal life but also a lasting
personal relationship
with God starting the moment
you ask Jesus so save you.

When Jesus returned from the grave;
he had overcome death;
and because he overcame death,
he has the power to lift us from
the grave and give us eternal life.

Jesus gives us Himself when we accept him.
He can do that because he has the power to infuse
us with Himself.
To live intimately with
God and enjoy his company,
we need Jesus to infuse us with Himself,
and this can happen.

Believe and accept Jesus as our
raiser from the dead,
and we will have the eternal life promised
in the New Testament.

Jesus overcame death and
hell and now sits on God's right hand in heaven.
No other great leader can claim this position.
God has made Jesus the only way to heaven.
Jesus said, *"I am the way, the truth, and the life.
No one can come to the Father except through me."*
John 14: 6.
New Living Translation

God requires us to believe in Jesus and accept
him. God has never acclaimed any other
faith leader as his beloved Son or claimed any of
the great prophets as sons.
It is Jesus whom God has invested
in to gain the worship of the
race of people he created for himself
but which was tragically lost by Adam and Eve.

It is essential to accept Jesus into the centre of
our very being, our heart.
But are we ready?
Are we convinced that Jesus is the way,
the life, the truth?

God is speaking to you,
the reader,
to take that step and commit and become a
new person and the recipient of eternal life and
enjoy a relationship with Him.

God is waiting lovingly in the wings for the moment you decide, and he will begin
to pour his deep peace, joy, and provision into you.
Why wait?
Why waste any more time when we could be enjoying the presence of a mighty, loving God?
That moment could be now.

Here is a prayer to pray to accept Jesus as our Saviour. *"Father, I'm sorry for my sins.*
I believe Jesus died to forgive my sin.
And I receive that forgiveness.
Jesus, I make you, my Lord.
I believe you are alive and that you now live in me.
Thank you, Jesus, for saving me.
I turn from my old life and ways
and will follow you from now on."

If you have prayed this prayer
from the bottom of your heart,
then know that God has accepted you,
that you are now his child,
and that there are no barriers between
you and God because Jesus
has come into your heart and lives there.
Your acceptance of Jesus
has put you in God's good books.
God has accepted you unconditionally as you are.

When you prayed this prayer from your heart,
you were born again.
There was no fanfare or flashing lights,
just a quiet sense of cleanness,
well-being,
joy,
and peace
that came into your heart.

The truth is:
You are now a new person.
Your spirit has been born again.
On the inside, you are a new person.
*"My old self has been crucified with Christ.
It is no longer I who live, but Christ lives in me.
So I live in this earthly body by trusting in the Son of
God who loved me and gave himself for me."*
Galatians 2: 20; New Living Translation.

You are now right with God.
God has forgiven your rejection
of him in the past;
in fact,
he has forgotten your rebellion
and has made you anew.
It is no longer you that lives but Christ in you.
Today you have been born again;
you have the gift of eternal life.
God has given you many more advantages,
but He will show you them as you grow in him.

Now that you have been born again,
you will find
many of your old likes and dislikes will disappear,
and new desires and thoughts will begin to
emerge
to foster the new you,
the Jesus in you.
The habit of reading
your Bible should become a daily habit.
The Bible is God's voice;
through it, he will guide you and tell
you his will and the direction he wants you to go.

Don't start to read the Bible at the beginning.
Begin to read the
Gospel of John in the New Testament.
This Book starts us off in our new life with Jesus.
Then go on to read the other gospels.

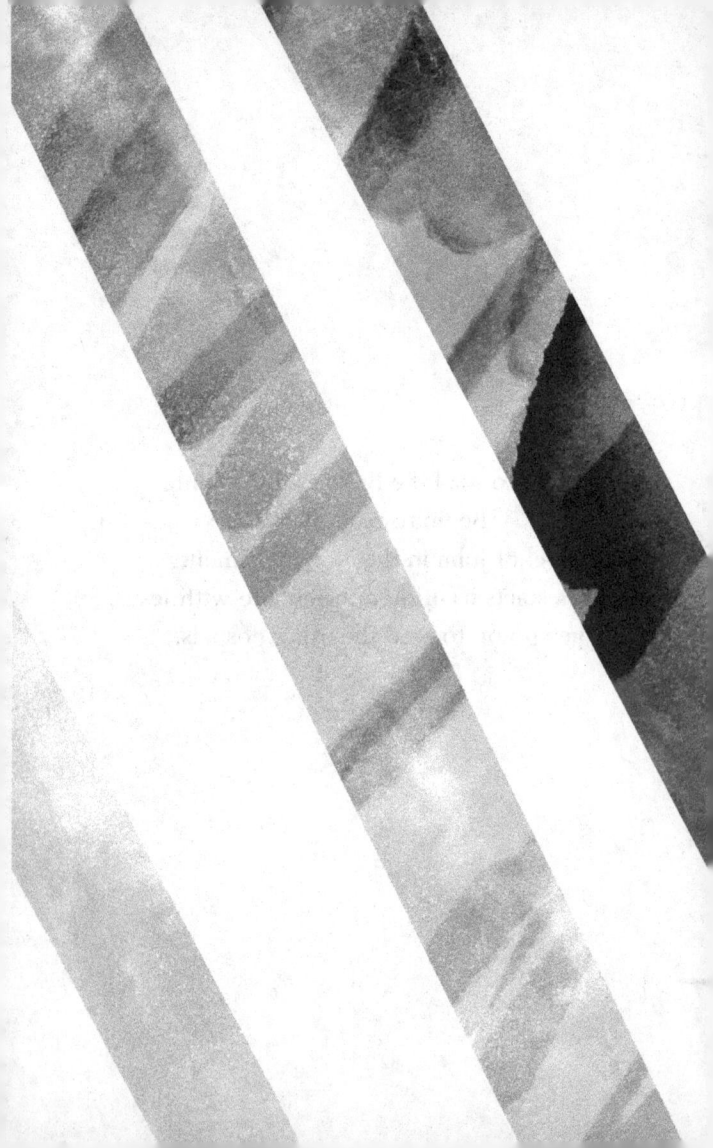

At some stage,
you can go back and begin
to read the Bible from the beginning.
There are many translations of the Bible;
for ease of reading and understanding obtain a
copy of the New Living Translation.

Maybe you have never prayed in your life;
well, talk to God as if he were next to you.
Remember, Jesus dwells in your heart so you can
speak to him one-to-one.
Practise these two things daily;
you will experience great joy and peace.
Jesus explains,
"I am leaving you with a gift
— peace of mind and heart!
And the peace I give isn't fragile
like the peace the world gives.
So don't be troubled or afraid."
Living Bible.

You will experience a cleansing that no detox can achieve because
God has cleansed your conscience.
You will experience a conviction
when even contemplating doing
something that displeases Jesus in you.
Obey these convictions and grow in the Lord.

One last word,
the more you open your mind,
heart, and feelings,
in short, yourself to God,
the more he will fill you with himself.

A great relationship with God will develop.
You will know God intimately;
you will hear his voice.
Look to fellowship with other Christians,
and find a church that will
strengthen your relationship with God.

You can email me at gwen.leane@hotmail.com or call me on 0488166201 to talk more about your new life in Christ.

ABOUT THE ILLUSTRATOR

Kylie Leane lives in a little house, with her pet cats, Winter and Charcoal.
Between writing and drawing, she enjoys spending time at the gym, going for long walks, watching anime, playing a good video game, and curling up by the fire in winter.

She loves bringing stories to life and making beautiful books is one of her greatest passions in life.

Being dyslexic does cause some trouble, and self-publishing is one mountain after another, but the reward of telling stories is worth all the hassle.

kmlpublishing.com

www.ingramcontent.com/pod-product-compliance
Lightning Source LLC
Chambersburg PA
CBHW011148290426
44109CB00023B/2530